THE STORY OF THE DENVER NUGGETS

Aaron Gordon

Jamal Murray

A HISTORY OF HOOPS

THE STORY OF THE

DENVER NUGGETS

JIM WHITING

CREATIVE SPORTS

Lafayette "Fat" Lever

CREATIVE EDUCATION / CREATIVE PAPERBACKS

Published by Creative Education and Creative Paperbacks
P.O. Box 227, Mankato, Minnesota 56002
Creative Education and Creative Paperbacks are imprints of
The Creative Company
www.thecreativecompany.us

Design and production by Blue Design (www.bluedes.com)
Art direction by Rita Marshall
Production layout by Rachel Klimpel and Ciara Beitlich

Photographs by AP Images (Jeff Chiu, Don Emmert, David Zalubowski),
Getty (Andrew D. Bernstein, Bettmann, Dustin Bradford, Tim Defrisco,
Focus On Sport, Carl Iwasaki, Mark Junge, Mitchell Leff, Richard Mackson,
Doug Pensinger, Mike Powell, Dick Raphael, Jamie Schwaberow, Mike Stobe,
Damian Strohmeyer), NASjerseys (Dave Morrison), Newscom (Icon SMI),
Shutterstock (Brocreative, Andrey Burmakin)

Library of Congress Cataloging-in-Publication Data
Names: Whiting, Jim, 1943- author.
Title: The story of the Denver Nuggets / by Jim Whiting.
Description: Mankato, Minnesota : Creative Education | Creative
    Paperbacks, [2023] | Series: Creative Sports: A History of Hoops | Includes
    index. | Audience: Ages 8-12 years | Audience: Grades 4-6 | Summary:
    "Middle grade basketball fans are introduced to the extraordinary history
    of NBA's Denver Nuggets with a photo-laden narrative of their greatest
    successes and losses"-- Provided by publisher.
Identifiers: LCCN 2022007523 (print) | LCCN 2022007524 (ebook) | ISBN
    9781640266247 (Library Binding) | ISBN 9781682771808 (Paperback) | ISBN
    9781640007659 (eBook)
Subjects: LCSH: Denver Nuggets (Basketball team)--History--Juvenile
    literature. | Basketball--Colorado--Denver--History--Juvenile literature.
Classification: LCC GV885.52.D46 W457 2023 (print) | LCC GV885.52.D46
    (ebook) | DDC 796.323/640978883--dc23/eng/20220604
LC record available at https://lccn.loc.gov/2022007523
LC ebook record available at https://lccn.loc.gov/2022007524

Kiki Vandeweghe

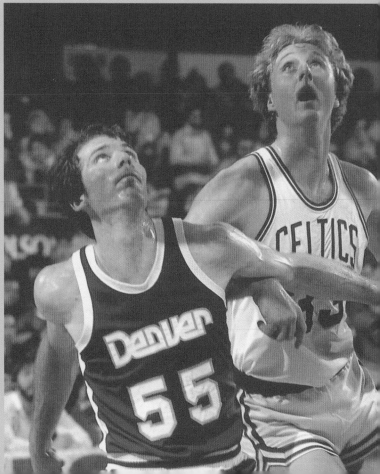

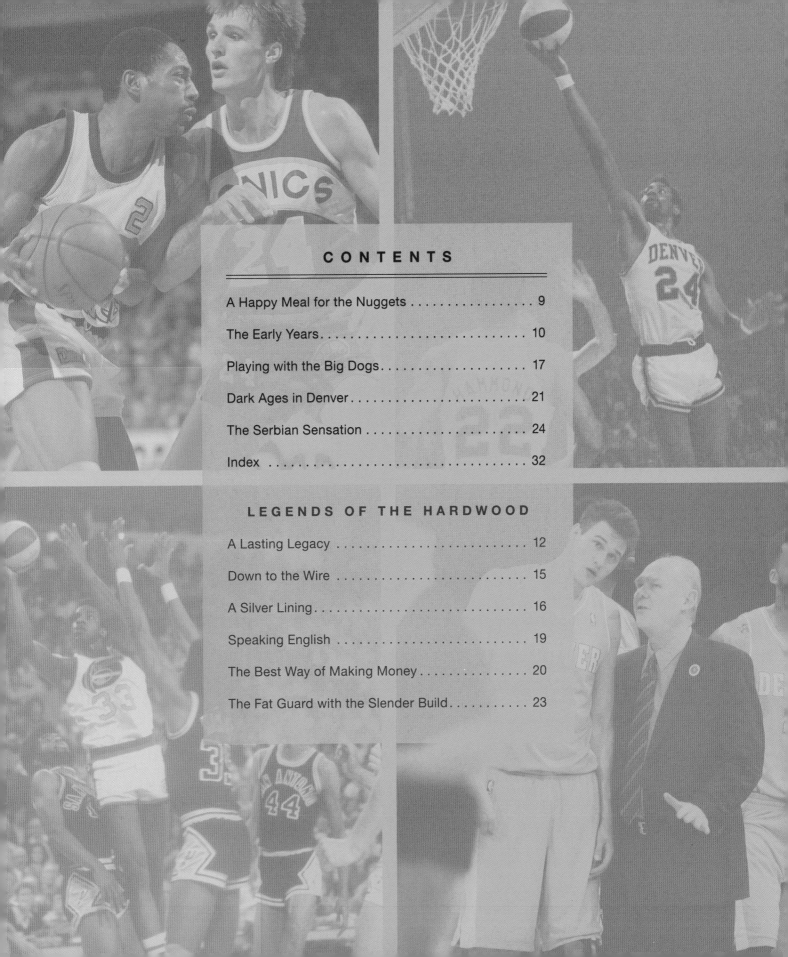

CONTENTS

LEGENDS OF THE HARDWOOD

1989 - Barcelona Jugoplastika vs. Denver Nuggets

A HAPPY MEAL FOR THE NUGGETS

The 1989 McDonald's Open was full of high-octane hoops. In the tournament, one team from the National Basketball Association (NBA) played a mini tournament against three elite European clubs. The Milwaukee Bucks and Boston Celtics of the NBA won the first two tournaments in 1987 and 1988, respectively. Now it was the Denver Nuggets' turn.

Much more was at stake than just another exhibition game. NBA commissioner David Stern popped into the Denver locker room before they played against Barcelona, who was the reigning champion of the Spanish League. "You guys are doing a great job," Stern said. "It's time to go out and play—and you guys better not lose." The Nuggets got the message. They romped to a 69–40 halftime lead and cruised to a 137–103 victory. "They [Barcelona] were exhausted and just gave up," said Denver coach Doug Moe. "But Jugoplastika [the European Champions Cup winners and their next opponent] is a very good team. It will be another story for us on Sunday."

Moe was right. Jugoplastika's roster included Tony Kuko and Dino Rajda, two future Basketball Hall of Famers. The Nuggets had a reputation for scoring a lot of points. They glided up and down the court. So did Jugoplastika. "They played as good an offense as the best NBA teams," said Moe. "They scored at will. It was like layup practice."

Nevertheless, the Nuggets opened up a 15-point third-quarter lead. An intense Jugoplastika rally narrowed the margin to a single point late in the game. Denver guards Lafayette "Fat" Lever and Walter Davis each tallied six points to ensure Denver's 135–129 victory and win the tournament.

Jugoplastika may have lost the game, but it won in a larger sense. Within a few years, dozens of European players joined the NBA. This influx of talent has grown even stronger in recent years. Denver is one beneficiary. For the past few seasons, Serbian center Nikola Jokić has been at the center of their success. In 2021, he was voted the league's Most Valuable Player (MVP). He was the first Nugget to receive the honor. He won the honor again in 2022.

THE EARLY YEARS

Professional basketball in Denver dates back to the NBA's first season in 1949–50. One of the teams was the Denver Nuggets. The nickname reflected the region's mining boom in the 19th century. People swarmed to Colorado. They hoped to find nuggets of gold and silver. But no swarm of fans found the time to watch these Nuggets. The team had an 11–51 record. They stopped playing after just one season.

The current Denver franchise traces its history back to 1967. It started as a member of the American Basketball Association (ABA). The league was developed to rival the well-established NBA. Denver businessman Bill Ringsby had the controlling interest. He named his team the Rockets.

That same year, power forward Wayne Hightower left the NBA's Detroit Pistons to play in Denver. Speedy point guard Larry Jones was playing in the Eastern Basketball League. He wanted to play in the ABA. He wrote to every ABA team. Denver was the only one that responded. It was a good move. The two players combined for an average of 40 points a game. The Rockets went 45–33 in their first season. But they lost in the first round of the playoffs to New Orleans. The following season was nearly the same.

Larry Jones

ABA ALL-STAR GAME
MCNICHOLS ARENA
DENVER
JANUARY 27, 1976

Wayne Hightower

A LASTING LEGACY

ABA officials wanted the league's last All-Star Game to leave a lasting impression. It did—though not because of the game itself. "We were sitting around the office one day [before the game], discussing things that would draw more people, and it just came to us—let's have a dunk contest," said ABA executive Jim Bukata. The contest took place during halftime and featured five of the league's highest flyers. Each were judged on five different dunks. It came down to the Nuggets' David Thompson and Julius Erving of the New York Nets. Erving won. Fans loved it! The NBA reintroduced the contest again 1984. It has become one of the best-known events of the NBA All-Star Weekend.

Both leagues drooled at the prospect of forward Spencer Haywood. At age 19, he had been the leading scorer for the 1968 U.S. Olympic gold-medal basketball team. Now the college sophomore was looking to make it in the pros. At that time, NBA teams could not draft players until their class graduated. The ABA didn't have that rule. Denver drafted Haywood before the 1969–70 season. He led the league in scoring (30 points a game) and rebounding (19.5 per game). He was named ABA Rookie of the Year and MVP. After a slow liftoff, the Rockets blasted to the top of the ABA's Western Division. They beat Washington in the first round of the playoffs. But they fell to Los Angeles in the next round.

Following that spectacular season, Haywood joined the Seattle SuperSonics, who offered him more money. Without Haywood, Denver had just one winning season in the next four years.

By 1974, the ABA was in financial trouble. The two leagues decided to merge in 1976. Several ABA teams joined the NBA. Denver was one. But the NBA's Houston team was also named Rockets, so Denver needed a new name. Team officials reached back to the team's original roots. They chose Nuggets.

The team made another important change. Larry Brown became coach. In the final two years in the ABA, the Nuggets went on a winning streak. They soared to an ABA-best 65 wins in 1974–75. A vital member of the team's rise was rookie Bobby Jones. He led the league in field goal percentage while averaging nearly 15 points per game. Denver beat Utah in the first round of the playoffs. But Indiana tarnished the season by defeating the Nuggets in the second round. Nevertheless, the team captured the hearts of local fans. "Larry Brown probably saved the Denver franchise," said Nuggets center Dave Robisch. "There was serious apathy about the basketball club."

There was no lack of interest in the 1975–76 season, the last of the ABA. The Nuggets' 60–24 record again topped the ABA. Fans poured into the new McNichols Arena. They wanted to watch high-flying rookie swingman David Thompson's spectacular dunks. Thompson was nicknamed "Skywalker" for his incredible jumping ability. "The whole measure of vertical leap began, I think, with David Thompson," Chicago Bulls guard Michael Jordan said. "He vaulted off the ground—exploded off the ground." The team also traded for burly center Dan Issel. "The Horse" added toughness under the basket. In the ABA Finals, the Nuggets faced the New York Nets, who had another player known for aerial acrobatics: Julius "Dr. J" Erving. The Nets won, 4 games to 2. Game 6 was the final one in ABA history. Could the Nuggets run with the "big dogs" of the NBA?

Bobby Jones (24 in white)

DAVID THOMPSON
SHOOTING GUARD
HEIGHT: 6-FOOT-4
NUGGETS SEASONS: 1975–82

DOWN TO THE WIRE

For all his brilliance, David Thompson never won an individual scoring title. He came close in 1977–78. He trailed George Gervin of the Spurs by 14 points going into the season's final day. Coach Larry Brown encouraged Thompson to shoot any time he was open. He scored an NBA-record 32 points in the first quarter. He finished with 73. It is the fourth-highest individual point total in NBA history. However, Gervin won the NBA Scoring Champion title that year with an average of 27.22 points per game. Thompson averaged 27.15. It is the closest finish in NBA history.

DENVER NUGGETS

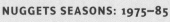

DAN ISSEL
CENTER
HEIGHT: 6-FOOT-9
NUGGETS SEASONS: 1975–85

A SILVER LINING

Dan Issel was a superstar in the ABA with the Kentucky Colonels
for five years. Then the owner needed cash. He sold Issel to the
Baltimore Claws. They never played a game. Issel was sold to the
Nuggets. He was unhappy. He had deep roots in Kentucky. "There
certainly were some hard feelings when I was sold," Issel said. "But
a year later, there was no ABA, there was no Kentucky Colonels, and
I was in a pretty good spot." Issel became Denver's second all-time
leading scorer. Eventually he was selected for the Hall of Fame.

PLAYING WITH THE BIG DOGS

Yes. The Nuggets could run with the big dogs. Denver had a stellar start in the NBA. Bobby Jones was a key reason why. He was stellar on both ends of the court. He was named to the All-Defensive First Team all four years with the team while leading the league in field goal percentage three times. The Nuggets won 50 games in 1976–77. They lost in the conference semifinals but came back the following season and advanced to the conference finals. They lost to the Seattle SuperSonics, 4 games to 2. Then Brown left. Jones was traded. Denver struggled without their seasoned coach. The team had losing records for the next two seasons.

In 1980, the Nuggets began laying the groundwork for success. They hired Doug Moe as coach. Players liked his laid-back style and sense of humor. Guard Elston Turner was surprised at how Moe conducted drills. "Some of the guys had their practice gear on, some had raggedy-looking sweats, and some even wore jeans," he said. "Doug would sit on the sideline . . . making jokes with everybody, while all the players were doing their own thing." The Nuggets also made one of their best-ever trades. They acquired small forward Alex English. He joined Thompson and rookie forward Kiki Vandeweghe to form a run-and-gun offense. Moe's strategy was to focus on the offense and scoring points. It worked. Denver led the league in scoring in 1980–81. Unfortunately, their defense couldn't stop opponents from scoring too. Denver won just 37 games.

The team went into overdrive in the following season. The Nuggets averaged 126 points a game! It is the highest average in NBA history. They won 46 games in 1981–82 but were eliminated again in the playoffs.

Denver won 45 games in 1982–83 and advanced to the conference semifinals. The win total dropped to 38 in 1983–84. Denver still made the playoffs but lost yet again in the first round. The Nuggets traded Vandeweghe. "It was a trade you had to do no matter how much you liked Kiki," Moe said. "We were able to get some players we really needed." One was Lafayette "Fat" Lever. He led the Nuggets to a 52–30 record in 1984–85. They lost to the Lakers in the conference finals.

The Nuggets won 54 games in 1987–88. That was their best mark since joining the NBA. A key factor was guard Michael Adams. He stood just 5-foot-10, which was exceptionally short for basketball. "He has to sneak around and through the big men, a mouse in a living room filled with big cats," wrote Leigh Montville of *Sports Illustrated*. "His little-kid jump shot, lifted from his hip as if the ball weighs 50 pounds, is a heave." The Nuggets advanced to the conference semifinals. They lost to the Dallas Mavericks. Denver squeaked into the playoffs the following two years. Both times they were swept in the first round.

Michael Adams trading card

ALEX ENGLISH
SMALL FORWARD
HEIGHT: 6-FOOT-7
NUGGETS SEASONS: 1980–90

SPEAKING ENGLISH

Alex English was quiet and soft-spoken. "I'm not so flashy, not so boisterous," he said.
"I'm low-key. My job is to do the job I'm supposed to do. There are people who don't see it,
but they aren't paying attention." Those paying attention know that English is Denver's
all-time leading scorer. He was named to eight All-Star teams. His Nuggets jersey number 2
is retired. English was the first player to score 2,000 points in eight straight seasons. Some
people call him "poetry in motion." That is appropriate. He has published several books of
his poetry. He also starred in the 1987 film *Amazing Grace and Chuck*.

DENVER NUGGETS

DIKEMBE MUTOMBO
CENTER
HEIGHT: 7-FOOT-2
NUGGETS SEASONS: 1991–96

THE BEST WAY OF MAKING MONEY

When Dikembe Mutombo began playing college basketball at Georgetown
University, coach John Thompson gave him some advice. "Son, you
will make millions and millions of dollars more than people who score
if you can play defense," Thompson said, "which means two things—
rebounding and blocking shots." Denver desperately needed someone
with that skill set. Mutombo didn't let them down. He was selected to
the All-Star Team as a rookie. Whenever he blocked a shot, he wagged
his index finger to mean, "No, no, no. Not in my house." He went on to
become one of the greatest defensive players in NBA history. He is also
noted for his humanitarian work. He has donated millions of dollars to
improve living conditions in his native Democratic Republic of the Congo.

DARK AGES IN DENVER

ew owners took over the team in 1990. They fired Moe. He had led the team to nine straight playoff appearances but no championship win. Lever was traded. The Nuggets released English, who was disappointed. "I had envisioned that I would go out like Dan Issel and Julius Erving, that I would make the trip around the league and get to say goodbye to all the people in all the different cities," he told reporters. Adams tried to pick up the slack. He averaged 26.5 points with his "little-kid heaves."

The Nuggets struggled. They won just 20 games in 1990–91. They traded Adams. They weren't much better the following two seasons. But they had drafted 7-foot-2 center Dikembe Mutombo in 1991. The Nuggets improved just enough to earn a spot in the 1993–94 playoffs. They upset top-seeded Seattle in the first round. This marked the first time in NBA history that an 8-seed defeated a 1-seed. After losing the first three games to the Utah Jazz in the second round, they won the next three. But Utah took Game 7. Denver won 41 games and lost 41 in the following season. They were swept in the first round of playoffs.

No one could have foreseen what happened next. The Nuggets struggled to a 35–47 mark in 1995–96. The next season they slid to 21 wins. In 1997–98, they won a mere 11 games. It was nearly the worst record in NBA history. They won only 14 the following year. The Nuggets climbed to 40–42 in 2000–01 but then tumbled backward in the next two seasons. But things were about to change.

LAFAYETTE "FAT" LEVER
POINT/SHOOTING GUARD
HEIGHT: 6-FOOT-3
NUGGETS SEASONS: 1984–90

THE FAT GUARD WITH THE SLENDER BUILD

Lafayette "Fat" Lever was anything but fat. The slender guard weighed only 170 pounds.
He received the nickname "Fat" from his younger brother who had problems saying all the
syllables in his first name. The nickname stuck throughout his playing career. His career
started in Portland, where he averaged just shy of nine points per game over two seasons.
Denver acquired him in a trade before the 1984–85 season. His game really flourished in
Denver. In six seasons, he averaged 17 points and 7.5 assists per game. He was an All-NBA
Second Team selection in 1986–87, when he led the league in triple-doubles with 16. The
Nuggets reached the playoffs in all six of Lever's seasons in Denver. They reached the
conference finals in 1985. Lever's number 12 now hangs in the rafters of Ball Arena. It is
one of only seven numbers retired by the franchise.

THE SERBIAN SENSATION

Denver drafted Carmelo Anthony with the third overall pick in the 2003 NBA Draft. As a freshman, he led Syracuse University to the national championship. In just his sixth pro game, 'Melo became the second-youngest player to tally 30 points. Four months later, he became the second youngest with 40. Denver returned to the playoffs for the first time in nine years. It lost to the Minnesota Timberwolves.

Midway through the 2004–05 season, Denver had a disappointing 17–25 record. George Karl took over as coach. The Nuggets went 32–8 the rest of the season. They made the playoffs, but again lost in the first round.

The Nuggets thrived under Karl's direction. But they continued to exit the playoffs early. "It's disappointing," said Anthony. "All you got to do is try to come back next year and try to start all over again." They did more than "start all over again" in 2008–09. Denver soared to a 54–28 record. It was the team's best mark in 21 years. The Nuggets cruised through the first two rounds of the playoffs. But they couldn't get past Kobe Bryant and the Lakers in the conference finals.

Before the 2010–11 season, Anthony refused to sign a contract extension. Denver traded him. They still made the playoffs. But they lost in the first round to Oklahoma City. The Nuggets led the league in scoring in the following lockout-shortened season. Once again, they were defeated in the first round. Denver shot to a 57–25 record in 2012–13. It was the best in team history. "That Nuggets team, devoid of a single All-Star player, wasn't even supposed to make the playoffs," wrote Mark Knudson of *Mile High Sports*. "Karl was voted NBA Coach of the Year

Carmelo Anthony

because he led a roster of spare parts to 57 wins." But the Warriors bounced the Nuggets in the first round of the playoffs. Karl asked for a contract extension. Team officials didn't just refuse—they fired him. Like Moe, he had taken the Nuggets to the playoffs for nine straight seasons without a single championship.

Without Karl, the Nuggets dropped to 36 and 30 wins the following two seasons. As the 2015–16 season got underway, the Nuggets had high hopes for rookie center Nikola Jokić. "Jokić is so good at getting deflections and steals," said new coach Mike Malone. "We're so excited about his progress and his potential." But the Nuggets finished with just 33 wins.

They nearly made the playoffs in 2016–17. Jokić was runner-up for the NBA's Most Improved Player Award. Point/shooting guard Jamal Murray was MVP of the Rising Stars Challenge Game. The Nuggets went over .500 for the first time in five years in the following season with a 46–36 mark. Along the way, Jokić notched the fastest-ever triple-double in NBA history. It took him just 14 minutes and 33 seconds. But Denver fell one game short of making the playoffs.

There would be no more near misses. Denver won 54 games in the 2018–19 season. Jokić was named to the All-NBA First Team. The Nuggets advanced to the second round of the playoffs. They lost to the Portland Trail Blazers in seven games. The 2019–20 season was suspended for more than four months due to the COVID-19 pandemic. When play resumed and the playoffs began, the Nuggets overcame a 3–1 series deficit in the first two rounds and won. No team in NBA history had done that during the same playoff run. They advanced to the conference finals against the Lakers. They fell behind 3–1. There would be no comeback this time.

Nikola Jokić

Will Barton

Jokić started 2020–21 with four triple-doubles in the first six games. He ended it with his first MVP selection. Second-year small forward Michael Porter Jr. more than doubled his scoring output from the previous season, adding an average of 19 points per game. Denver defeated the Trail Blazers in the first round of the playoffs, but the Phoenix Suns swept them in the next round.

Jokić did even better the following season. His average points per game increased from 26.4 to 27.1. And his average rebounds per game increased by a whopping three per game. He was named NBA MVP for the second straight season. The team hovered around the .500 mark in the early part of the season. Then they began winning consistently. At one point they won 28 of 40 games and finished 48–34. They faced Golden State in the first round of the playoffs. Unfortunately, both Murray and Porter were injured and didn't play. The Warriors won the series, 4 games to 1.

In more than half a century of pro hoops, the Mile High City has yet to notch its first championship. But Nuggets fans remain optimistic. With a combination of good drafts and good trades, they hope that their team will someday strike gold.

Michael Porter Jr.

INDEX

Antonio McDyess